The New Message of Love, Book 2

Journey to Love

Moriah

Copyright 2019 All rights reserved.
ISBN: 978-0-9709461-3-3
International Institute For Human Empowerment, Inc.

Dedicated to the Provider of Unseen Assistance

With appreciation:
Book cover: Erica Shipe Dodd, B.F.A.
Layout and design: Jody Morgenegg, CustomWebCare
Editing: Ruth Kellogg, Ph.D.

The New Message of Love was recorded as received from the Teachers of Love over a period of 30 years. These highly evolved angelic beings speak through their Messenger named Moriah. It is now time to make the Message public.

You can learn more about The New Message of Love:

Book 1 Invitation to Love
Book 2 Journey to Love
Book 3 The Healing Journey
   Available on Amazon.

See also:
www.thenewmessageoflove.com
www.enterthenewworld.com
www.newworldempowerment.com
www.newworldempowerment.org
www.humanempowerment.org

Facebook pages:
Moriah
New World Empowerment Center
New World Empowerment Ministries
Moriah's New World Library
International Institute For Human Empowerment

Facebook Group:
The New Message of Love

Note to the Reader

The story of Moriah is a human story filled with Experience. As the Experience grew, the story became more than human. It is a story of connection: heaven and earth; seen and beyond seeing; heard and beyond hearing; information, and knowing beyond information; separation and joining.

It is the story of a little girl born in an isolated area of a lesser-known state in the United States. It encompasses this life, but also previous lives of preparation. It is the story of the evolution of a soul that took on its final relevance in this incarnation.

It is the story of connection, at first unrecognized, and of building trust with unseen Guidance. Of losing faith only to regain it with Experience. It is communication across boundaries of species, time, death of the body, and geographical location. It is learning about the connection of consciousness which is the sea in which All exist. It is realizing that consciousness-awareness is knowing the experience of life without a body. It is non-local. And most importantly, it is real.

The New Message of Love does not promise riches; it promises that what is needed will be provided. It does not promise status; it promises service. It does not promise worldly success; it promises successful evolution of the soul.

You did not come here for riches or status. You came to learn, to heal, and to serve. In other words, you came to love. Most of all, you came to Be Love in the world.

And so, it is.

Journey to Love

Introduction

Journey to Love is the curriculum for joining. Joining is required for all in order to return to Love. Therefore, as one takes each Step, one is reminded that Beings in all realms are taking these steps, too. As Humanity begins the task of consciously choosing to accept the Invitation to Love, each then is responsible to take the Steps of the Journey to Love. As others take these Steps also, you will be guided to accept one another without preference. Journey to Love will take you along a path toward acceptance of all Beings, Human and Non-Human. That is how your worlds will merge safely through the evolution that is occurring.

Beings, Human and Non-Human, travel a similar path. Once the need for Love is recognized within the soul, the desire to fulfill that longing begins. Humans tend to become confused, and attempt to fill themselves with the treasures of the world: promises of eternal youth and beauty, wealth, fame, excitement, and perfect health. As they strive for these worldly promises, they may abuse their health, families, and well-being. They are prone to overindulgence of those things that make them happy in the moment, or reduce pain. The pain of the void that is created may lead to extreme behaviors to quell the longing: alcohol, drugs, fast mobile craft, affairs, and illnesses of excess. All are attempts to quiet the longing and fill the Love-shaped vacuum that eventually becomes unbearable. All of these efforts are in vain, for only Love can fill the void.

Humans often give voice to wanting Love, or God, while giving little priority to this endeavor. Love waits. Love is patient. Love is energy that does not force Itself. Instead, Love waits for the opening, the crack, the voice that welcomes It in. It enters quietly at first. As Its presence is acknowledged, and as the spiritual sojourner desires, It moves into the open and painful places of one's life. It clears chakras, opens minds, challenges old beliefs, encourages action, and begins to move one to more awareness of Its presence.

As this Presence begins to take residence within one's soul, one hungers for more. Hunger and thirst, and the attempt to fill with overindulgence in food and drink, is really the Love-desire. That is also why many on the spiritual path begin to change their diets and daily activities, focusing more on healthy food and beverages, meditation, exercise, and wholeness of mind-body-soul. It is this consciousness of self-care that prepares one for the greater journey of returning to Love. Journey to Love is for the spiritual sojourner who has become more aware of caring for the body as a temple; is accepting of the Invitation to Love; and is ready to take the daily Steps of Journey to Love.

Joining is the immersion into Love. Love energy, once accepted, guides one to follow Love. Love guides decisions, empowers the weak, overcomes loneliness, and leads one to a life of service and fulfillment.

Joining is what you might call miraculous in every way. It fills the heart's longing for more. It prepares the soul to retire much of the unfortunate and useless information it has gained while in the body. It reminds one of what was known before coming to earth. It clears away the biases and prejudices one has learned. It prepares the sojourner to see each person as a soul with a body, rather than a body with a soul. It leads to detachment from the physical, and movement through faster vibrations for the soul. But none of this may be accomplished without the faithful discipline of the Steps, in Journey to Love.

You have come here because of previous preparation. All of this was necessary for you to be able to make the commitment to Love. Surrendering to Love is Step 1, and the most essential step. It is only when you give yourself totally--your desires, ego, need to control, fear--that you are then ready to accept Love as your guide in all decisions.

Love will lead you on a path of greater fulfillment than you could ever achieve in your worldly pursuits. It will calm the aching in your heart. It will bring you to relationships that work to fulfill Spiritual Purpose. It will give meaning and direction. It will cause you to experience deeper love relationships than you thought possible. And it will slowly dissolve your desire for the glitter of the world.

Glitter, through things that tempt you with desire, will lose its hold on your life. You will find new meaning, and new ways to express that meaning. Your heart will be full of love and you will desire to serve according to your Purpose as it is revealed to you. Journey to Love is both a journey and a destination. Be not afraid. Journey to Love is that for which your soul deeply longs. This longing cannot be filled by the world. Attempts to do so will lead to disappointment, failure, loss of faith, illness, and eventually death. Death of understanding is an expensive price to pay to remain isolated.

It is the acceptance of the Invitation to Love, and the subsequent Steps of Journey to Love, that will bring you to Peace.

JOURNEY TO LOVE -- PART I
"THE PREPARATION"

Journey to Love is the journey to God. It is the spiritual path that takes one from a position of being in the world, to a position of being in the world but not of the world.

The Journey to Love is a journey that is inclusive. All are invited. No one is excluded. The invitation is given to all that all might begin the most wondrous journey Home.

Home is God. Home is where we have come from. Home is that to which we will return. Yet there is much that must be accomplished before we can return Home and remain enjoined. All who return Home are enjoined. They are one. They will never again experience separation. Separation is the return from Home to the earth plane to learn and to contribute one's gifts. One experiences many incarnations until one is ready to join. Thus, all joining occurs until one returns Home.

Many are joining, yet there are many who cannot make the decision to join. They must be lovingly released by those who began the journey to Love. Therefore, the first step in journey to Love is the process of becoming unburdened. All will be left behind that all may be given. That which is no longer essential will be returned to the world. All that is essential will be taken on the journey. Therefore, one may not exist at both levels.

As one moves from the level of the world to the level of the spiritual path, one takes a step in one's own evolution and the evolutionary process of the world.

All that is needed will be provided. All that is essential will find inclusion. Yet the step onto the spiritual path is a step of faith as it requires one to release what one has to receive the unknown. Yet the unknown contains all that the heart desires. When one enters the earth plane, one is brought into contact with much that is not essential. Those things of the world that one has been led to believe lead to success do not fulfill the
vacuum in the heart. The heart can only be filled with that which it recognizes. Therefore, those things it does not recognize, do not bring fulfillment.

Relationships are brought into proper alignment for the one on the spiritual path. Those relationships that are not essential will fall away. Those which are essential will be brought into one's path. One will need to become most alert, and be prepared to relinquish all that is not in alignment with one's spiritual path. It is a requirement that cannot be understood at the initiation of the journey. Therefore, one must desire God above all. One must return to God through the Journey to Love. The Journey to Love provides all that is essential for the return Home.
As you begin the journey by accepting the invitation to Love, you will meet others who will draw you toward them. They may be supportive of your spiritual journey, or they may tend to pull you off the path. You must be most discerning and committed. You must desire the spiritual path above all. All decisions, all relationships, will be based upon their ability to be supportive of the

Journey to Love. You will begin this journey by a decision to commit time to meditation and practice.

This practice is essential to the journey. In other words, one cannot return Home without the journey, and one cannot be on the journey without practice. Therefore, one must accept that one is worthy of the self-discipline essential to devote one's time to meditation and practice.

There will be many obstacles along the journey. There will be many steps that will be most difficult. Yet by relying upon one's inner guidance one may move through all obstacles toward Home. The journey will be most complete. Yet it must be one's priority. One may not say, "I will be here" and go there. In other words, it will require one's full attention and focus.

The one on the spiritual path becomes focused. They carry a Presence which polarizes all with whom they come into contact. Those who desire God will be drawn to them. Those who cannot yet begin the journey will be repelled. Therefore, as one begins the journey, one must begin to be discerning. One must develop communication that is at deeper levels so that one might be protected from those who cannot join until they are ready to receive the invitation.

We will begin by developing discernment and learning true communication. Therefore, we will begin with a lesson on true communication.

Directions: Pages entitled Notes are provided after each lesson for recording insights and experiences. In addition, keeping a private journal is recommended.

Lesson #1

Today I will 1 learn how to truly communicate. True communication is not dependent upon verbal exchange, action or body language. These forms of communication are visible and/or audible. True communication occurs at a level that is neither audible nor visible. It occurs at a vibratory level that draws or repels. It occurs in all life. It is not limited to human and animal forms. It is available for humans, for animals, for the combination, yet it is also available with all that is living. This includes plant life, and it includes humans and other beings who are not of your kind.

As your world evolves, there is much mixing of those of many cultures and languages, and communication is most challenging. Yet true communication exists at levels that do not require verbal, visible, and audible understanding. They occur at a level that is vibratory, and this level will either bring joining, or it will repel those attempting to join into different directions.

As you move into the vicinity of that which is living, you will be drawn, or you will be repelled. There must be no emotion. There must be only acceptance. Acceptance will be that the other is able to join or unable to join. If the other is able to join, you will move forward in your attempts to initiate further communication. However, if the other is unable to join, you must move away as it will be essential for your own protection to do so.

One can practice true communication in all aspects of human endeavor. One can note the reactions that are visible, verbal, and audible, and note whether they are in alignment with the vibratory messages one is receiving. In other words, one may say the right words, yet one may have a distinct feeling that the other is being deceptive.

One may hear the words, "I love you", yet note actions that are not in alignment with the words. One may see one who appears most loving, yet who is unable to say the necessary words because of background and former experience. Therefore, one must begin by developing one's ability to discern whether the messages being received at a vibratory level are consistent or inconsistent with what is occurring in the interaction.

Daily Practice

The lesson for the first week is: in all areas of interaction with others note whether these actions, either verbal, visual, or audible, are in alignment with the vibratory messages one is receiving. This must occur in all interactions throughout the day.

These interactions may be at work, transitions between home and work, at home, during times of entertainment, and during times of intimacy. In other words, all interactions are to be examined for alignment between communication at the level that is verbal, audible, and visible, and the messages at a deeper level that one is receiving. Allow 20 minutes for reflection at the end of each day, and keep a diary of all interactions. Note your response with each interaction. At the end of the day, during the 20-minute practice period, white a short summary of the interactions that occurred.

Complete the activity with a Meditation that begins: "I am open to communication at all levels and I seek that assistance which will enable me to clarify all interactions so that I may learn discernment. I recognize that discernment is essential for the journey to Love, and I willingly accept all that is revealed to me. Thus, I begin the spiritual Journey to Love with the recognition that discernment in communication will assist me to remain on the spiritual path. I will not judge another, yet I will be open to examining each interaction that I may learn and prepare my contribution to the world."

Notes

Lesson #2

Communication is a way of joining. It provides the means to bring those who view themselves as separate, together, in the highest level of communication you call intimacy.

There is a union of self so that two become one. Intimacy is more than physical joining. The purest level of intimacy is joining at the levels of mental, emotional, physical, and spiritual. When that occurs simultaneously, there is union that is like the joining of one with God.

Joining is the greatest desire one has. All of life on the earth plane is an attempt to join. The joining of lovers, or parent and child, contain all four levels of joining. Other relationships generally contain at most three, as all cannot physically join. Yet there can be joining by touch, by birth, by sexuality.

This complete joining is a union that all desire, yet the romance in your culture leads to joining that is incomplete. It relies upon physical and emotional joining. It sometimes includes mental joining, yet there is not an emphasis on spiritual joining.

Spiritual joining is more than religious joining. In your world, people frequently join because they are, as they say, of a similar faith or religion. Yet this is not true spiritual joining though it may include spiritual joining. In other words, spiritual joining is much more than a tendency toward similar belief patterns. In order to unite spiritually, each must be on a spiritual path, moving in concert with the other. In other words, they must work at spiritual practice, and they must be able to respond to spiritual experience.

They must be able to support one another's growth and they must be able to serve as validators for one another. In other words, joining spiritually is not stagnant. It is movement along two individual paths that are joined.

True intimacy occurs when there is joining at every level. This is the highest level of intimacy. Though there are other levels that may also be enjoyed, they will not provide the fulfillment each is seeking. When you find true intimacy, you are married already. In other words, the marriage already existed. One does not choose marriage; one discovers marriage. And once marriage is discovered, one will not be able to find fulfillment with another.

When true intimacy is discovered, it creates much disruption in the lives of those who have discovered it together as they are often in other relationships. This creates much pain and guilt as they are not able to understand why they must leave their current relationship for another. Yet when one discovers marriage by experiencing true intimacy, one cannot return to the previous stage without much pain and suffering. One must leave one's former life behind to join the one with whom one was previously committed. True marriage begins before entrance to life on the earth plane.

Daily Practice

Consider for one week your current relationships. Determine if you are joined spiritually, mentally, emotionally, physically. Look without judgment at your primary relationships to discover the level of intimacy you experience. Write about each level in each relationship. Be honest and share this with no one who could be injured by the sharing. In other words, find another who can be most objective and understanding, and who can maintain confidentiality. Consider whether your primary relationship supports your spiritual practice and provides the intimacy essential for your evolution so that you may contribute your gifts to the world.

Begin your 20-minute meditation with the affirmation: "I acknowledge my evolution beyond the earth plane. I acknowledge that I have entered the earth plane to learn and to contribute. I acknowledge my desire for true intimacy."

Notes

Lesson #3

Communication is the means of relationship between two or more beings. This communication may be verbal, action, body language, and vibrational. It can occur at any one level or at many levels simultaneously. It can move from one level to multiple levels and continue that movement back and forth. In other words, it is not fixed.

As you encounter others, it is important to learn the communication needs and to begin to understand each communication level and combination of levels. Each may mean different things in different circumstances, and these circumstances may be cultural means of communication used by that society and may also reflect the origin of that particular being. In other words, communication is a means of relating between two or more like or unlike beings. This can become most confusing when one considers the many variables, yet it is at the vibrational level that most communication occurs.

Communication at the vibrational level is found between and among human beings, animals, plants, and any combination of these. It also occurs in those instances when one encounters beings of other realities and other worlds. It is through the vibrations of thoughts and emotions that true communication occurs.

As one begins to study this intricate system, we call communication, one must begin to learn in small segments. It can be most overwhelming to try to deal with communication in a broad sense without considering the parts. Therefore, we will begin practice by considering, for the period of one week, verbal communication between two or more human beings.

Daily Practice

For one week, at the end of each day, write down the names of all with whom you had verbal communication. You may also consider keeping a list throughout the day as this may assure that there are no omissions. However, do not comment on any of the communications until you begin a reflective period of 30 minutes to review the communications of the day. Look for similarities. Look for differences. Consider whether or not you were speaking on the phone, or you were receiving simultaneous body language by being present with the person or persons.

What was the emotional tone?

Did it change throughout the conversation?

What did you feel was really being said?

What was the tone of the communication?

Did it invite you to communicate again, or did it tend to close off possibility of future communication?

Was it a communication that was complete in itself or did it require follow-up?

Was it with a friend, or one you did not know?

Consider these and many more variables, and look for underlying information that was not spoken yet which you acquired. Make notes about the communication, and note how much communication occurs without words.

Begin your 20-minute meditation with the following affirmation:

"I am a student of true communication. I desire to know the beings with whom I am relating. I am learning to communicate what I truly desire to communicate by learning to understand communication from others. I will learn true communication so that I can truly join."

Notes

Lesson #4

Communication is love made manifest. Love cannot exist where there is no communication at any level. Therefore, the desire to join is made possible through communication, and communication allows one to accept the invitation to join.

Communication brings together those with much familiarity, with some or little familiarity, and with no familiarity. In other words, communication is the bridge that joins from the initiation of relationship through profound relationship should that occur. Communication provides the context for joining. Yet that communication may be made manifest in many ways.

We will begin by considering communication that is verbal. This communication may be with those of comparable language development in the same language, within a similar language yet of different levels of ability to use the language, and it may be between those of different languages where there may be no understanding of the other language, or some understanding. The communication is on a verbal level and utilizes a language as the vehicle for joining.

When two people speak the same language, they use many words that have a variety of meanings, and there may be confusion as to the meaning being assigned to the word. In others words, language is made up of symbols you call words, and these symbols may represent one thing for one person and something different for another. Therefore, even between those of comparable ability in the use of a common language, there may be misunderstanding due to the meaning associated with each word. Two people may speak to one another, and each may think that they have communicated adequately, yet the message received may have a different interpretation. Therefore, what has been the intended communication has not been received.

Daily Practice

We will begin to study communication between two of comparable ability of a common language. For a period of one week, list the people with whom you have verbal communication, and at the end of each day, review those communications:

Were they complete?

Do you feel that what you tried to communicate was received?

Were you careful to present the information in more than one way to allow for understanding?

Did you check for understanding by asking the other for their understanding of what you said?

In this lesson it will be important to begin to understand whether what you are attempting to communicate is in fact that which is received. Begin your 20-minute meditation with the following affirmation:

"I desire to communicate with others as a vehicle for joining. I recognize the importance of expressing my thoughts in ways that can be understood by another. I will check for understanding and will be willing to change my way of expressing to meet the needs of the one who is receiving my communication. I will be willing to use a variety of opportunities and strategies to ensure that the message has been accurately received. I understand that it is my responsibility to express my thoughts in a way that can be accurately received."

Complete the meditation with this affirmation: "I am open to communication at all levels, and I seek that assistance which will enable me to clarify all interactions so that I may learn discernment. I recognize that discernment is essential for the journey to Love, and I willingly accept all that is revealed to me. Thus, I begin the spiritual journey to Love with the recognition that discernment in communication will assist me to remain on the spiritual path. I will not judge another, yet I will be open to examining each interaction that I may learn and prepare my contribution to the world."

Notes

Lesson #5

Communication that is received from another is open to many interpretations. These interpretations may be based upon ability to communicate within the language. Therefore, when one uses words that are unknown to another, clarification as to meaning is required. It is also true that words that are used even most commonly carry many different meanings, and these meanings also are each open to interpretation. Therefore, there are many opportunities for inaccuracy and incompleteness. It is essential to check
for understanding of another's communication. When you receive a communication, it is most important to rephrase that information to ascertain whether you have correctly interpreted what you have received.

Daily Practice

During the day note everyone with whom you speak. At the close of the day, review each interaction:

Did you repeat the information you received in at least one other way to check for accuracy?

Did you ask for clarification when the meaning received was not the same as what was intended?

Did you continue to seek clarification until a common understanding was reached?

Did you have a feeling of unity with the other at the moment that true understanding was achieved?

What were your feelings at the moment of understanding in each verbal transaction?

Begin your 20-minute meditation with the following affirmation:

"It is my responsibility to check for understanding for any communication that I receive. I will seek to fully understand the other, even though I may not agree with their opinion. I recognize that in relationship, understanding of position is of more importance than agreement. Therefore, I will ensure that in every verbal transaction, I understand what is being communicated. I will indicate that understanding though I need not indicate agreement. It is this understanding rather than agreement that provides unity."

Notes

Lesson #6

Communication is that which will bring all to God. Not all who communicate will return, yet those who choose to return do so through communication. Therefore, communication is the vehicle for this returning to occur.

There are many occurrences in your world that will require you to be calm, and capable, in the area of communication. These occurrences include the movement of your people resulting in the mixing of many cultures; the economic interdependence, which is becoming more apparent to you; and the societal changes requiring the combination of resources of many of your institutions. In other words, those areas that formerly allowed separation and independence, will now require interdependence.

There are other changes that are occurring simultaneously. You are being visited by Others not of this Earth. While intelligence is understandable to you, the lifestyles and ways of existing and surviving are unknown to your people. Therefore, as these Beings who are more highly developed, and therefore able to more easily travel to your planet, increase their visitations, there will be occurrences where there will be a mixing of Beings of different planets. This mixing will require communication, yet it cannot rely on communication as you have known.

The communication that will be essential for understanding another of another planet will require that you be able to communicate on all levels. That is why you are beginning a curriculum in communication.

We have been working with you as you study communication between two of a similar language with comparable ability and without comparable ability within this language. Yet you will need to begin to be aware of communication on all levels. There is also much variation within each level.

Daily Practice

We will continue our study by noting facial expressions in those verbal transactions of two of common language. This will include those of comparable verbal ability, and those who are not of comparable ability. In other words, it is important to begin to note facial expressions in all transactions when one can be seen by another. During the day, note all verbal transactions that occur when you could see one another. At the end of the day, review transactions, noting facial expressions.

Did the expression seem consistent with the message you were receiving?

Did the expression seem to convey a different message from the one you were receiving?

Was there enthusiasm? Was there apathy? Was there pain? Was there delight?

Was the other trying to convince you to join in his or her view point?

Note this and many other possible reactions. As you move through the weekly lesson, note whether you are becoming more aware of the facial expressions of the other at the time of the transaction. Begin to note whether the facial expression is consistent with the message, or appears to be giving a different message. If so, what is the other message?

Begin your 20-minute meditation with the following affirmation:

"I seek to know and respond to every communication. I desire to know the true meaning of the communication, and then become open to what is occurring on other levels. I will listen with both my ears and my eyes as well as my feelings to be able to respond to the communication that is really occurring. I desire to emanate love through communication, and this can best be done by developing communication that can hear and respond to all levels. Therefore, I commit myself to the study of true communication that I might be able to facilitate the changes that are occurring. My service to God, or Love, will be through the development of true communication."

Notes

Questions for Reflection

1. Who are the people who support my spiritual journey?

2. From whom can I receive more support?

3. What do I need to feel supported?

4. Who or what is blocking my support?

5. If I could have the ideal situation to evolve spiritually, what would it be like?

6. Describe the best experience I have had that supported me mentally, emotionally, physically, and spiritually.

Notes

JOURNEY TO LOVE -- PART II
"THE JOURNEY"

In our deepest times, faith is challenged. Words and songs of religious life may appear shallow in the face of fear of death. Your people live by faith. They have often designed their worship time to be preacher/teacher-centered. While some wisdom may
be shared, it is the heart of the individual person that opens, or closes, to Love.

When you came to earth, you still retained some memory of that time between lives you call heaven. As you moved forward into your daily experience of the world, new memories developed, and old memories before life on earth faded. They are lost or
forgotten now, but will return upon your return! In other words, when you return Home, you remember Home, and your worldly memories fade. What remains of life on earth is connections which continue until your next assignment. At that point, your earthly assignment is complete, and you are free to remember and reconnect with loved ones.

It is true that the coming and going of souls from one assignment to another causes feelings of loss as ones' missions now briefly diverge. One continues his/her mission on earth, while the other moves forward to reflect, remember, renew, and move to one's next lessons. Thus, the lessons of life are but a few at a time, each within a new assignment.

Each lesson builds upon previous learning. Thus, the one on a spiritual path continues the Journey to Love.

You are a channel of Love and Peace through eternity, but first you must Love. The Journey to Love begins here. You are ready. It is now time.

Note:

The Steps in Journey to Love are given here as received in order to retain authenticity. It is important not to be turned off toward the authoritative tone, but to recognize that the Guidance given is the path for your journey. At times the language may seem awkward. This sacred text is delivered as received for your highest benefit.

Directions:

Each Step is to be done daily for one week. You will note that some of the Steps suggest writing your responses. You may choose to record verbally rather than write if that is your preference. It is important to record in such a way that responses are always available for your review. A blank page for notes is included for convenience and easy reference. It is suggested that you find a special time and place for your daily meditative Step. A quiet place, adequate soft lighting, and items that are meaningful and enjoyable to you can support your experience. It is also important to keep your notes or recorder easily accessible to capture ideas as they come to you.

As you move forward with Steps, you may begin to notice a sense or feeling of energy or Presence. Your Meditations may become a place where much becomes known to you. The Spiritual Path is full of Experience.

Experience takes you more deeply into intuitive knowing and understanding. As you progress you will move beyond simply faith, to knowing through Experience. The **Journey to Love** is a deepening of spiritual experience, guidance, direction, fulfillment, and peace.

WEEK 1   STEP 1

This Step is to be done daily for one week.

Open your heart to accept Love. Ask in prayer that Love come into your soul and bring you fulfillment and peace. Say in prayer that you are ready to begin a new life in Love with these words:

"I surrender myself to Love. I ask that Love guide me in all decisions. I ask for strength to detach from my former desires that were unhealthy and not fitting for my Path. I ask that those relationships that support my Journey become apparent, and that those unable to support me fall away. I release them with love. Make me Your person in the world that I might serve in the ways that I am uniquely designed to serve. Make me a Channel of Your Love and Peace through eternity."

Notes

WEEK 2   STEP 2

Now that you have surrendered to Love, asked for Guidance in all decisions, and made the commitment to follow Love in all your life, it is time to evaluate your current situation. Take a sheet of paper and divide into 2 columns. Column one is a list of those people who will support your new Journey. Column 2 is a list of those people who are unable at this time to support you.

After reviewing each list, place the paper out of sight. Meditate daily with the following prayer:

"These people who are my friends may or may not be able to support me in my new Journey. I recognize that to be strong, I will require support. Now let those who can support, come forward. Allow those who are unable, to fall away. Support me through this challenging time, that I might not resist, but that I may be able to release with love all who are unable to support my journey. Let everything I do be done for Love."

Notes

Over time those who can support the one on the Spiritual Path will move into prominence, while those who cannot make the Journey will begin to fall away. Assess your interactions during the past 7 days. Reflect upon any persons who have moved forward in support. Acknowledge those who have experienced difficulty moving forward with you. How do you know that those who appear to support you are truly able to commit to that assignment? How do you know those who are unable to support you? What evidence do you see? At this time you may see someone unexpectedly come forward in support. You may also note that there are others moving away. Allow this to occur without resisting.

Each day after reflection, pray:

"Help me to accept that not everyone will be able to support me. May I not attempt to convince nor sway them. Instead, may I accept their decision with love. I recognize that as my vibration shifts, those who are pulled toward that vibration will also shift. It is a spiritual truth that vibrations attract other like vibrations. Those who cannot engage or accept this increased energy will fall away. Help me to resist the desire to control. Help me to accept that all is going according to the Plan."

Notes

WEEK 4   STEP 4

You are now beginning to note a shift in what holds your interest. You desire stillness and peace, and long to avoid disruption and drama. Those relationships that are unable to support you are falling away. Whether by a gentle drift, or a fiery angry split, the ability to move forward on the Spiritual Path has taken precedence. You may feel a longing for old relationships. Resist the urge to run after those that have moved away. See who comes forward. When you are consciously on the spiritual Journey to Love, you are never alone. When in meditation, daily, ask for the following:

"The path is sometimes lonely and I may feel afraid. Yet, I acknowledge that I am never alone, for Love is always with me. Love is an energy that pervades all. It holds one close when afraid, holds one up when challenged, holds one back when angry. Love heals old wounds, and takes up residence where wounds once were. Let Love be my Guide in all decisions."

(A page for your notes has been added for your convenience. You will also need a notebook and pen for all of the following Steps. A recording device may be substituted as long as all previous responses can be easily located and reviewed.)

Notes

WEEK 5   STEP 5

Spiritual purpose is beginning to emerge. As you release old desires for the glitter of the world--social life, ambition, competition, status--in favor of personal time for reflection, new issues and desires will emerge. Dreams of long ago may arise. Memories of past interests may again begin to come to the fore. Certain people, activities, or publications may trigger unexplained desires for creativity. A need to express through art, music, writing, or other art form may surface. Follow these desires to again express that which has long been repressed. Do not judge these impulses. Simply follow, and note whether they hold any purpose in this new life.

Each day in meditation, with pen and notebook (or audio recorder) beside you, ask:

"What do You want me to do?" After a brief reflection, write anything that first comes to mind.

Notes

WEEK 6   STEP 6

Review what you have written on each of the past 7 days. Note any repetition, if it exists. From where do you think each idea originates? Write what you feel each response means. Each day in meditation, ask:

"Why am I here? What do You want me to do? I know that my life has Purpose, and I desire to fulfill that Purpose. Please reveal to me that which remained hidden in my past, so that I may bring forth my Purpose in the world. I know that I am uniquely designed to serve."

Each day, write, without judgment, any thoughts that come to you.

Notes

WEEK 7   STEP 7

Review all of your written or recorded responses. Ask, "What am I to learn from this?" Write whatever first comes to mind. Repeat daily for one week.

In meditation each day, pray: "Help me to understand my Purpose. Guide me as I reflect and write. Help me to hear internally. Lead the way that I might follow. 'Make me an instrument of Your peace.'"

Notes

WEEK 8   STEP 8

By now you are noting that some of your friends have moved away. Others have come forward. New people have arrived in your life. Some friends will take interest in your thoughts. Others will feel that you have become "too serious." Still others will appear to withdraw, or question your actions. This is a natural part of spiritual awakening and commitment. All that is not necessary will fall away. All that is needed will be provided.

In meditation daily, reflect upon those few with whom you feel close, even if they are new friends. Ask that your relationships that support your Spiritual Purpose become more pronounced, and that those who are unable to support you may be released with love. Ask that you be able to release all--people, activities, and material items--that you might move forward on your path.

Notes

WEEK 9   STEP 9

As you move more deeply into your spiritual practice, Journey to Love, you may begin to question, "What will I be asked to do? What will I be asked to give up? Who will I need to release?" This is a somewhat painful, sometimes euphoric time. Emotions may run from depression to anger, to sadness, to joy. It is a time of spiritual cleansing. As you relinquish all that cannot go with you on this Path, recognize that you are never alone. Your Teacher Guides go before you, to prepare your way. They assist you when you are weak. They rejoice with you at each Step accomplished.

In Meditation each day, pray:

"I am never alone. The Teachers of Love prepare, guide and assist me at all times. I will always have the strength to do the Steps if I first call upon Them. I will begin each Meditation with the words, 'The Teachers of Love are with me.'"

Notes

WEEK 10   STEP 10

Some days you may feel deeply committed to following your Spiritual Path. Other days you may become distracted with the activities and demands of daily life. Select a symbol that will be your reminder that you are never alone, and that the Teachers of Love are with you. Place that symbol in a variety of places as a reminder. This will help you to increase your awareness at all times of day of your spiritual journey.

In each daily meditation, set the intention to be consciously on your Spiritual Path at all times. Say, "I intend to be constantly consciously aware of my spiritual commitment, and my spiritual journey, including all that will be revealed."

Notes

WEEK 11   STEP 11

Spiritual experience is direct personal experience of a unique event. This may include feeling, knowing, seeing, hearing, touching, and other little-understood intuitive events. Each person has unique gifts which only truly emerge after commitment and practice. These events are not to be feared, but to be accepted as part of the unfolding of spiritual understanding.

In each daily Meditation, ask that what is needed be provided. Ask to increase your capacity to accept spiritual experience.

Say: "I am open to spiritual experience and the lessons that will be provided. I call upon the Teachers of Love for protection, guidance, and understanding."

Notes

WEEK 12   STEP 12

Reflect upon any unusual experiences you may have had. These are experiences that others may attempt to explain away, but for which there appears to be no rational answer. Write down each unexplained event, and note your age, reaction, and what it meant to you. Each day, as you reflect, remember when others' attempts to "explain away" this event caused you to deny or forget the experience.

In each daily Meditation, ask for those unexplained life events to come forward in your consciousness to be written down, and reflected upon.

Say, "Thank You for this life I have been given. Thank you for events that have brought me to this place on my Journey. Reveal to me those events that I may have forgotten, but which influence my direction. Help me not to be afraid, but to open to new possibilities."

Notes

Each day, begin to meditate for a few minutes. Stop meditating, and write down any thoughts that come to you. Do not judge your thoughts as they arise. Simply write, and do not stop the flow.

In Meditation, say:

"I ask for the Teachers of Love to be with me now, and at all times. I ask for whatever I need to know to be revealed to me as I write. I give thanks for this Guidance. I will work to understand more each day."

Notes

WEEK 14   STEP 14

Journey to Love is the guidance from the Teachers of Love to bring each person into union with Love. Love is God. Love is Higher-Power. Love is the Source. Love is energy in all Beings. As you do each Step with deep desire and devotion, you will be brought closer to that complete union. Allow nothing to keep you from Love. Love heals. Love guides. Love moves you forward toward your unique Purpose in the world.

In Meditation each day, ask:

"Take away anything that would take me off my Spiritual Path. Make the way clear. Hold me in Love. Guide my steps daily. 'Make me an instrument of Your Peace.'"

Notes

WEEK 15   STEP 15

As you proceed on your Spiritual Journey, see who can support you. Who can help you? Who understands? Who cares? Make a list of those people with whom you can share your true desires and dreams.

In daily Meditation, ask the following:

"What do You want me to do? Who can help me?" Write your responses as they come to you. At the end of the Meditation, review what you have written.

Notes

Finding a time and a place where you are not distracted is essential for the Spiritual Sojourner. Where can you be alone with your thoughts? Consider where you can go at least once per week for a few hours of silence. Here you might write, meditate, paint, draw, walk, or find solace. Here you will be able to hear the inspiration that comes to you. Lack of distraction from people and events is essential for the Spiritual Sojourner to continue to advance. Make a list of those places where you can be alone with your thoughts and expressions without distraction.

In Meditation each day, say: "Thank You for the spiritual awareness to which I have opened. I am aware that I need time alone to be able to continue to grow. Guide me to where I can find opportunity for spiritual experience and expression. 'Let all I do be done for Love.' "

Notes

You are now aware of places, environments, where you can be alone with your thoughts. Keep a notebook to record your thoughts and insights at all times. When you go to bed, keep your pen and notebook beside you to record dreams, experiences, inspiration, or new awareness. This is the true beginning of a lifelong interaction with Love through your Teachers. You will need to always have a way to record inspiration as it comes to you. Now that you are becoming open, that inspiration may come to you at all times and spaces as long as you remain open to listening internally.

In Meditation, say:

"Thank You that I am growing in spiritual experience and my ability to receive guidance. I know that this will continue as long as I remain open to receive. Help me to stay on my Path, and follow my Steps daily. Thank You for all that has been revealed, and all that is about to be revealed to me."

Notes

WEEK 18   STEP 18

Spiritual growth and development are much like growth and development of a child. If nurtured daily, it will grow and develop in positive ways. If neglected, it will fall into difficulty. It is time to make a life commitment to follow Spiritual Purpose where it leads. This is a divine moment. Choose something that will be symbolic of this commitment that you will keep with you daily. Some people have chosen a ring, symbolizing their commitment to Love.

In Meditation daily, ask that an appropriate and special way to reflect the commitment you are about to make be revealed to you. Say, "As I prepare to make a spiritual commitment of my life to follow Love where It leads, I ask that ideas of an object that symbolizes my commitment be revealed to me. Guide me always that I may be your instrument of peace and love."

Notes

WEEK 19   STEP 19

    Review all of your writings to date. Notice any repetitious words or phrases. Write these down. Make a list of all thoughts that seem to be especially relevant to you on your Path.

    In daily Meditation, say: "Thank You for the words and ideas given to me. Help me to remember, understand, and grow into what You have uniquely designed for me."

Notes

WEEK 20 STEP 20

Some of your friends are less attentive. Some may have dropped away. Your primary relationships are those that can support you, or take you off your Path. Note especially your spouse, significant other, boyfriend or girlfriend, or best friend. This relationship is the one most likely to support you, or keep you from following your path. Examine closely this primary relationship. Make a list of those qualities you like, and those you find difficult to accept. Ask of each characteristic, "Why do I like this? Why does this quality make me uncomfortable?" Note any qualities you may find unacceptable.

In Meditation, say, "I desire to stay on my Spiritual Path. I recognize that I will require relationships that support me. I ask that only those relationships that can support me flourish, and those that would take me off my path, fall away. I ask for strength to help me through this process."

Notes

WEEK 21   STEP 21

As your relationships shift, new areas of disagreement may appear. Step back objectively and ask yourself, "Is this disagreement of importance to me? Is it a symptom of our pulling away?"

In Meditation, ask that what is necessary to this relationship be revealed to you as needed.

Notes

Grief is a product of loss. When those people who may have been right for us are no longer able to support us, this can be one of life's most painful experiences. Holding on to that which no longer serves our needs spiritually can take us off our Path. Releasing with Love can help us through this step. Although the other may react in pain and lashing out, you can find comfort in the peaceful acknowledgement that it is time to move forward alone on your Spiritual Path while remembering that you are never alone.

In Meditation daily, ask: "What do You want me to do? Give me strength to move forward alone, in the knowledge that I am never alone."

Notes

WEEK 23   STEP 23

Develop the habit of Presence. This is to cultivate the conscious awareness that you are constantly in the Presence of Love. Love is not something to be called upon only at special occasions or even relegated only to daily meditation and prayer. Practice several times daily with the thought, "And every word a prayer." This is the consciousness of constant Presence.

In Meditation daily, say: "I desire to live daily in the Love consciousness. Make every thought, interaction, word, a prayer that Love is with us and guides us. We are never alone."

Notes

WEEK 24   STEP 24

You are now realizing that Presence is with you with thought. You may feel or sense Presence when you think of Love, or Teachers of Love. There is an invisible connection between thought and Presence. Therefore, only you can deny the presence of Presence. Love is not pushy. It comes in when invited. It becomes a more constant awareness with practice. As you continue your daily Meditations through Journey to Love, this Presence will make Itself more apparent to you. Only you decide your Path, and only you can make the decision for lifelong commitment.

Meditate daily, asking that Presence be present with you. Ask to be able to sense Presence, and to be reassured that Love is always with you.

Notes

WEEK 25   STEP 25

You are learning not only to call upon, but to call in Presence, or Love. This is a result of continuous meditative practice and deep desire for Love. Love knows your heart. Love fills a vacuum in the heart that nothing but Love can fill. Begin each daily Meditation activity by asking Love to be present with you. This can be done silently, internally. This is inviting the constant presence of Presence.

In daily Meditation, give thanks for the Invitation to Love. Acknowledge your deep desire to continue to grow in spirit and in truth.

Notes

WEEK 26 STEP 26

Progressing on the spiritual path may take many twists and turns, yet the Path can serve to steady and center you. Since you began this Path, what events have occurred in these 26 weeks? How did you react to each? Is your reaction different from what it used to be, or would probably have been? Write and reflect upon each, including any that may be occurring at this time.

In daily Meditation, ask to become centered and react from a place of Peace. Say, "In all things and at all times, may I be an instrument of Peace."

Notes

WEEK 27 STEP 27

"You are a channel of Peace and Love through eternity..." This is that to which a spiritual sojourner aspires. Bringing peace and love to worldly pain and suffering is our mission and deepest desire. People go through periods of personal and family loss, accidents, and illness. These are among the greatest of human challenges. Bringing peace to suffering is how the spiritual sojourner enhances quality of life for others. This service may take many forms, but the essence is the same.

Consider where you are drawn to serve. What were your dreams? Did they become forgotten in everyday stressors? List those dreams you once had. Do not judge them to be inappropriate or silly. Within those dreams may be a truth of who you will become. Make lists. Reflect. Write anything that comes to you

In Meditation ask to know: "What would You have me do? What is my Purpose in the world?"

Notes

WEEK 28   STEP 28

Your life on the spiritual path is more like a puzzle than a strategic plan. You are designed to follow, rather than create, the Plan for your life. The Plan already exists. Through spiritual practice, meditation, prayer, practicing constant Presence, you receive each step only after the previous step is complete. Some steps take longer if the lesson requires more time to be learned. Therefore, your progression depends upon completing a step on your path, and understanding the lesson of that step.

In Business, you may have been asked to develop a 5-year, or long-term plan, and steps to achieve that plan. On the spiritual path, you complete your current step, and the next one is revealed to you.

In daily Meditation, ask the Teachers of Love: "What is my next step?" Write down all insights as they were received.

Notes

WEEK 29   STEP 29

Letting go is one of the challenging lessons that is repeated frequently on the spiritual path. At any moment you may be attempting to let go of an idea, material object, lifestyle, location, relationship, child, money, fear, control. Notice those things and ideas you find most difficult to release. That may give you an idea of where you are inappropriately attached. Inappropriate attachments may limit your progress on the Spiritual Path. List any areas where you feel you need to work toward releasing.

In Meditation each day, say, "I am eager to progress on my Spiritual Path. Reveal to me the areas where I need to practice release."

Write down those areas, and any thoughts that occur with them. Reflect and Meditate upon them during the week, adding others as necessary, and eliminating those that no longer control you.

Notes

WEEK 30   STEP 30

Trust is most important on the Spiritual Path. Often trust is given that is not deserved, and there are many negative consequences to the spiritual sojourner. Consider past relationships where you trusted, and then were betrayed or had your trust abused. List those people. Consider them individually. What was your gut telling you about that person before you trusted? What was your gut telling you about the relationship? Your intuition, or gut reaction, contains more information than you mentally process. While you may have assessed that this person was trustworthy, your gut may have been giving you important information that you ignored. With each name, consider if you would have trusted them had you listened to your gut reaction.

In Meditation each day, ask to develop your profound intuition, or instinctual response. Say, "Help me to grow in awareness of my instinctual response, my profound intuition. Help me to trust this intuition, and always compare it with my intellectual assessment in order to know who is worthy of my trust." Note any changes you are able to make during the week with this new awareness.

Notes

WEEK 31   STEP 31

Review your writings. What new awareness have you gained? What are repeated themes? Note all new awareness. Write down your questions regarding these lessons. List these questions in the order they feel most compelling.

In daily Meditation, say, "Thank You for new insights I have gained through Journey to Love. As I review each remaining question I have listed, I will listen for Your response."

Continue this practice by meditating for 1-2 minutes after reviewing a question. Quickly write whatever comes to mind. When the flow of the response stops or lessens, continue with the next question by meditating 1-2 minutes, and then writing the response,

Notes

WEEK 32 STEP 32

Review your writing from Step 31. As you read, more questions may emerge. Write each question down for further clarification. Meditate and then write the response to each question. If your responses were complete and you have no further questions, ask another question that is on your mind. Write the response. Throughout the week, write any questions that come to you, and meditate about each, followed by writing the response you receive.

Each day in Meditation, express gratitude for this wondrous way of questioning and receiving a response. Give gratitude that you now know that you are never alone.

Notes

A challenging but essential practice with channeled responses is to check that response against your gut instinct. Did it feel right? Did you feel that the response was independent of the answer you desired? Your fears and your preferences can influence and impact the answers you believe you are receiving. Therefore, it is essential for you to center yourself, and ask to be in a space of no fear and no preference. It is only when you have arrived, through meditation and practice, at being without fear or preference regarding the question or issue upon which you are focusing, that you may accept the answer as a true response.

In Meditation, ask (always) for the Teachers of Love to be present and guide you. Ask to be in a state without fear or preference. When you feel that centered space of equilibrium, then focus on the question and receive the response. Check the response against your gut, your intuitive instinct. Does this response feel right?

Use this process daily to gain spiritual guidance in all areas of your life.

Notes

WEEK 34   STEP 34

Your world is full of much diversity. As travel and mobility have increased, you may interact with many people of other cultures, and languages. It is not practical to learn every language, but it is essential to be able to communicate. Therefore, you will need ways other than words to communicate. This area of development is known as telepathy. It is not so much about reading others' thoughts, though some will become skilled enough to do so. However, it is essential to be able to acknowledge another's intentions, and to be able to acknowledge with confidence these intentions within yourself.

Every day for one week, note each person with whom you come into contact. Write down any information you gained about each that you learned without language. Did you notice their clothing? Did it give you ideas about their work or hobbies? Did they have distinctive characteristics? Did they wear clothing or jewelry that showed affiliation to marriage, organization, or philosophy? Did they have a regional accent? List everything that you noticed without communication through words or language.

In daily Meditation, ask to become more aware of others' intentions. Ask to increase your ability to sense information intuitively. Give thanks for all of your new awareness gained through Journey to Love.

Notes

WEEK 35 STEP 35

Consider all of the people you interacted with last week, and others that you met this week. These meetings do not require formal introductions. It could be at your school, community organization, place of worship, or place of business. With each interaction from these two weeks, consider, "Did I feel safe with that person? What characteristics did I note beyond what was learned through language?" List each person and what you learned about each beyond words.

In Meditation each day, ask to increase your awareness regarding others' true motives. Ask for protection through following your instinct and intuition. Ask for protection from any Other who might intend to harm you.

Notes

In Meditation we reach for the Beyond. We seek connection, protection, guidance, and reassurance that we are not alone. It is essential to understand that when dealing with what is invisible, we must always seek protection by our Angels, Teachers, or Guides, or whatever name with which you feel comfortable. These highly evolved Beings protect us from intrusion by other less-evolved Beings. It is important to ask for protection for ourselves and all our loved ones, including patients, students, and clients.

You now carry the Love energy. It is not welcomed by all. This can make you a disruptive presence. Therefore, ask for protection from any who might seek to hurt you or your loved ones.

In Meditation each day, ask for protection from any Beings, in sight or invisible, who might want to harm you or those you love and care for. Do this with each Meditation until it becomes a habit. Ask for protection before sleep for you and your loved ones. Ask that you continually be guided by Love in all situations, and at all times.

Notes

WEEK 37   STEP 37

As you go more deeply into meditative states, you may begin to have more frequent experience. Consider many of the religions of your world. Information was revealed to certain people, recorded, and these historical events formed the basis of religion.

Religion has much value in inviting people into the spiritual path. It has value in supporting the family through life cycles and events. Some find they need more, and move further into meditation, their spiritual Path and Purpose, and become open to spiritual experience. Spiritual experience is not static. It appears uniquely to the person, and is often life-changing.

What experiences have you had that are beyond explanation? Do you know others also having spiritual experiences? The new spirituality is based more upon one's own experiences and less upon another's experience. Therefore, your experiences of spiritual guidance, sense or feeling of Presence, hearing or seeing beyond what the physical ear or eye can perceive, will be the catalyst for your life lived with spiritual experience and understanding.

In daily Meditation, ask for guidance and understanding. Ask to be centered, grounded, and able to receive. Ask to have anything that does not support your spiritual path to fall away.

Notes

WEEK 38 STEP 38

Review your notes regarding what you noticed about individuals without language. Now move this observation to groups of two or more people. The collective consciousness of a group will have an over-riding or prevailing intent. For example, a group of people may not individually intend to hurt another, but if the over-riding intention is to hurt or damage another, the group consciousness, often referred to as group-mentality, may prevail over individual differences.

In your encounters, and in any televised events, what did you detect as the stronger or prevailing intent? Note your observations. What can you extrapolate from this? Does Love motivate people in a direction? Does fear motivate them in another direction? Record your observations and thoughts regarding each.

In Meditation each day, ask to be aware of the intentions of groups of people. Ask to increase awareness of each person and each group. Did you notice some reluctant to follow the crowd? Did you note some appear to be fearful at opposing the group intention? Ask for protection from any individuals or groups that might harm you, or those you love and care for.

Notes

In your society, some people are given deference due to education, status, wealth, or experience. Consider those in positions of power throughout your life including teachers, religious leaders, physicians, business executives. Make a list of powerful people beginning from your childhood, with whom you interacted. Consider each slowly and carefully. Were there teachers who loved children, and others who did not? What was the impact of a special teacher who loved you? What was the impact of a teacher whom you felt did not love you or another child in class? Do this activity over a two-week period, slowly examining each relationship. Consider your relationship with each of your parents separately. Write all that comes to mind.

In daily Meditation, ask for the ability to look at each relationship without judging yourself. Be completely honest about the impact each person had on your life, if any. Some will have had little impact; others may have brought joy or pain, self-confidence or lack of it.

Send love to each person, and thank them for the lesson learned.

Notes

WEEK 40　　　　　　　　　　　　STEP 40

Continue Step 39 all week. With each person you gained, or you lost, or both. Consider each person and write what was lost or gained next to each. Give yourself permission to be honest, as this is not to hurt another, but to recognize power in relationships, and to heal losses.

In Meditation each day, give thanks for those lessons learned, positive and negative. Ask to forgive them, as most were not aware of their power to hurt you. Ask for healing of the wounds you still carry. Give thanks that you now recognize great power of influence, pain, and positive impact. Ask, through Love, to be a positive influence for love in the world. Ask to be a Channel of Love and Peace through eternity.

Notes

WEEK 41   STEP 41

Review your relationships over your lifetime in which you had power over another. In childhood relationships, in school relationships, in personal family and business relationships, consider your power. What message do you want to convey to others? What do you want to contribute to the world? Meditate for 1-2 minutes, then write whatever contemplations and guidance you receive.

In Meditation daily, give thanks for your new awareness, understandings, and opportunities. Ask for blessings for all of your personal relationships. Ask that all that cannot support you, fall away. Ask that you be able to release them with love.

Notes

WEEK 42   STEP 42

Each day this week, write: "What do You want me to do?" Write the response.

In Meditation each day, ask for Love's will for your life. Ask to be purified that you might be a Channel of Love and Peace through eternity.

Notes

WEEK 43   STEP 43

Just as there is much diversity in your world, there is much diversity in the world that you are unable to see. Beings exist at every level and vibration. They also exist in a body on many planetary bodies, many of which remain yet unseen or unknown. Your intention is to navigate safely through the seen and unseen to fulfill your purpose. Your purpose is to serve on earth. Your purpose also is to assist in the evolution that is occurring.

Many have visited and continue to visit your planet. Those visitations will continue to increase until there is mixing of humans and non-humans. Communication through telepathic means will be essential. As you learn, and become more adept and more capable of expanded communication, so are other Beings. Many non-human beings are already capable of telepathy, and know your thoughts as well as intentions. Therefore, the following Steps will be to increase your telepathic abilities.

In Meditation daily, ask that you become more aware of others' thoughts and intentions. Use the skills you developed in previous Steps to receive guidance, and enhance your ability to be more aware of people and animals around you. Do they elicit Love or Fear in you? Ask that they elicit only Love from you.

Notes

WEEK 44   STEP 44

The remainder of this curriculum will provide you with the skills necessary to safely evolve. Change is constant now in your world. Whether or not you can perceive it, your world is constantly changing in all areas: climate, politics, geography, technology, communication, and energy. Therefore, you will need to:

1) Be centered

2) Be aware of change within

3) Be aware of outside change

4) Develop new skills for managing and/or navigating change

5) Employ new skills as needed

As you meditate daily, ask: "What do You want me to do? Help me to hear, see, feel, understand that which can only be known intuitively. Open me to new experiences. Guide my daily continuous development."

Ask: "In all situations and at all times, make me a channel of Your Love and Peace through eternity."

Notes

Practice becoming centered. Move to a quiet, accepting space, away from other's criticism and negativity. In a comfortable position, stand or sit with both feet firmly on the floor. Imagine a white light circling high about your head. As you focus, you imagine that circling white light descending slowly down to the center of the top of your head. As it descends, it picks up speed. As it moves downward, it moves through your body, through the head, neck, torso, and down your legs and into your feet. It pushes more strongly and quickly through your feet into the earth, where it continues to the inner earth's core. You are now in alignment with Love.

As you move forward each day this week, imagine that white light moving in concert with you, from far above your head, to the earth's core. Thus, you are centered, aligned with the Light of Love, and moving with protection through the world during all daily activities.

Repeat each day, moving in the conscious awareness that you move in Light at all times. At the end of each day, write whatever comes to you, whether observations, experiences, inspiration or any other thoughts. Repeat this entire process each day for one week.

Notes

WEEK 46   STEP 46

You are now in the forty-sixth week of this year-long curriculum. How have you changed? How have others changed in response to you? What change has been easy? What change has been difficult? What change has been painful? What change has been joyful? What feels different? What seems different? Do you feel confident? Assured? Open to experience? Less judgmental? Less fearful?

Each day following meditation, write your thoughts, positive and negative, about these changes. Do not judge your responses. Simply write and let these thoughts be revealed to you.

Notes

WEEK 47 STEP 47

Each day in meditation, ask to have these changes in the outside world since you began this curriculum revealed to you. Who has changed? What has changed? Do you know why it changed? What is changing now? What will be some future changes?

Ask that these answers be revealed to you as you write. Repeat this activity from the beginning each day for six days. On the seventh day, summarize the items from all six lists into one complete list.

Notes

WEEK 48   STEP 48

Trusting your own profound intuition is your biggest challenge. Even as you feel, think, even believe you know answers, your challenge will be to trust your own intuition to make wise and safe decisions.

Challenges will be presented to you this week in which you will need to make decisions without all of the information necessary. Use your profound intuition to make each decision that presents without adequate information. Write down each challenge, what you knew, what you didn't know, and what your intuition was telling you. What was the action you took? What were the consequences of the action? What was your intuition leading you to do? Was it the best choice? Did you experience doubt? Do you feel it was the best decision? Do this activity daily after saying the following in Meditation:

"I desire to learn the skills needed to navigate the world safely, even when I have inadequate information for a decision. Help me to learn to listen and follow wisely my profound intuition in all instances. Keep me safe in a confusing, changing world. 'Make me a channel of Your Love and Peace through eternity.'"

At the end of each day, review all consequential decisions you made. List each decision. Next to each decision, write Y for yes, and N for no. Did I rely upon intuition to make this decision?

Knowing what I know now, would I make the same decision again? Why? Why not?

Repeat this activity at the end of each day, beginning with Meditation, and incorporating the following words:

"Make me a channel of Your Peace and Love through eternity. Guide me safely through each day and each situation presented. Help me to see, hear, feel, and know internally. Guide me in all decisions, that I may one day guide others safely through the evolution that is occurring."

Notes

Practice for each of the next seven days what you know about each person on your path that day. Begin by listing each person, by name or description, on a page. Next to each one, write several comments about your perception of the person using only your intuition. (It is not necessary to record what you already knew or what they told you directly.)

At the end of each day, check to be sure that you were not responding due to bias. Note where you felt safe or afraid. Note any thoughts about the person that occurred when with the person, after parting from the person, and now reflection. What do you know intuitively that you did not know before?

Do this daily for 7 days, following Meditation. In prayer ask, "What do You want me to know about this person that can only be known intuitively?" Write the response.

As you go through the week, you will have several encounters with others. Some will be brief; some extended. Some will be with people well-known to you; others may be complete strangers.

In each situation, you will first realize new information using your skills of seeing, hearing, feeling, and intuiting. What do you know that is new? How did that new information influence your decisions? How did your decisions influence each interaction?

After you make a list of each person, write your responses to the above questions following their name. Leave plenty of space for responses as you now know much more intuitively about each.

Notes

WEEK 50   STEP 50

Your profound intuition about a person or situation can be greatly altered by your fears, including biases, and your preferences. It is essential be become objective in order to truly perceive what is really occurring. If you are afraid of certain people due to learned bias or past experience, recognize that bias or fear, and then mentally move away from it.

In other situations, or with certain people, you may desire a particular outcome. If you cannot recognize, and then step away from, that desire or preference, you will not be able to intuit objectively.

Consider mistakes you have made when relying upon your intuition. Did you deeply desire a certain outcome (such as, return to health in the body)? Did you have fear, such as prejudice due to race or religion? Did these fears or preferences cause you to be unable to objectively understand your own intuition? What was the mistake you made? What was the outcome?

Consciously review your intuition-based decisions each day beginning with this prayer in Meditation: "Help me to learn to receive information intuitively that can safely guide me, and others, through the evolution that is occurring."

Review your notes from Lessons 42-49. Each day write down the first 5 thoughts that come to you by asking: "What are the 5 things I learned today after reviewing lessons 42-49?"

Repeat for seven days, beginning each Meditation with, "What do You want me to know?"

Notes

This is an intense and productive Journey to Love that prepares you to navigate the changes you are facing, and will face. This preparation has been given to the world through Our messenger named Moriah. As you have taken each Step, the Lesson was prepared specifically for you. It is now time for you to move forward, supported by those relationships that are able to provide support; supported by the Teachers of Love who developed and shared this Preparation; and supported by Love. You will need to depend upon this support in all situations. Therefore, this week is devoted only to summoning and awareness of Presence.

In daily Meditation, ask that your Teacher Guides be present with you. Call them the name that has been given to you, or that feels right. You may also call upon the Teachers of Love. You are never alone.

After each Meditation, write whatever thoughts come to you. Write without judgment. Allow your thoughts to flow. Stop writing when the flow of words has stopped.

Notes

WEEK 52   STEP 52

This week, at all times, be grateful. List all that you are grateful for, beginning with the gift of life. Include family, friends, Guides/Teachers, experiences, and all with which your life is blessed.

Begin each daily Meditation with an expression of gratitude. Make a list of all you are grateful for that you can keep with you at all times. Refer to this list at the beginning of each hour you are awake for the next 7 days. You are developing the essential practice of living in gratitude.

"We, the Teachers of Love, are grateful for your openness and acceptance of this Preparation, Journey to Love. May it bless your life with direction, safety, peace and love."

Notes

DEDICATION

You are a Channel for Peace and Love through eternity. But, first you must Love. Love is of God. Love is God in Action. Love is Energy. Love is Force. Love moves ever forward, touching and gathering those who would respond. Think not that Love is for your own pleasure. It is for the returning of all to God. Therefore, let not your desire for pleasure be that which moves you forward. Allow Love to be the invitation to the feast. You are the manna for God. It is only when you give yourself completely as the sacrifice, that Love can be given to the world. Let all your life be a prayer that God will make you worthy of this sacrifice. For He sacrifices only those who are worthy and gives only to those who would receive.

Be not afraid, for sacrifice is the final union with God and none can take away its Joy!

www.ingramcontent.com/pod-product-compliance
Lightning Source LLC
Chambersburg PA
CBHW060158050426
42446CB00013B/2880